Images Free for use under the Pixabay Content License
Template created by Designrr
Printed by Amazon Inc.
First printing, 2024

Power Down: A Busy Person's Guide to Sleep and Relaxation

Power Down: A Busy Person's Guide to Sleep and Relaxation'" provides a structured roadmap to navigating the complexities of relaxation in a fast-paced world. This book is designed specifically for busy individuals who find it challenging to unwind and achieve restful sleep amidst their hectic schedules. Recognizing that time is a luxury for many, the book is crafted to offer quick, actionable strategies to help readers integrate relaxation techniques into their daily routines effectively.

The first section of the book focuses on understanding the importance of relaxation and sleep. It delves into the physiological and psychological benefits of restful sleep, emphasizing how inadequate relaxation can lead to stress, decreased productivity, and even health issues. This foundational knowledge sets the stage for readers to grasp why prioritizing relaxation is essential, even for the busiest of individuals. By presenting compelling statistics and insights, this section aims to motivate readers to make a conscious effort to incorporate relaxation into their lives.

Following the introductory overview, the book outlines practical techniques for rapid relaxation. This segment introduces a variety of methods, such as deep breathing exercises, mindfulness meditation, and quick stretching routines that can be performed in as little as five minutes. Each technique is explained in straightforward language, making it accessible for readers at any level. The focus is on simplicity and efficacy, enabling busy people to fit these practices into their daily schedules without feeling overwhelmed.

The third section of the outline is dedicated to creating a personalized relaxation plan. Here, readers are guided through the process of identifying their unique stressors and relaxation preferences. This self-assessment helps individuals tailor their relaxation techniques to suit their lifestyles. The book encourages the exploration of various environments—whether at home, in the office, or even while commuting—to discover the best settings for relaxation. By fostering a sense of ownership over their relaxation journey, readers are more likely to commit to the strategies presented.

The closing section emphasizes the importance of consistency and developing a routine. Establishing a regular practice of relaxation is vital for reaping the long-term benefits of improved sleep quality and overall well-being. This part of the book provides tips on how to integrate relaxation into daily life, including setting reminders, creating a calming bedtime ritual, and tracking progress. By reinforcing the idea that relaxation is not a luxury but a necessity, the book aims to empower busy individuals to reclaim their time and prioritize their mental health. Through this structured approach, "Power Down" serves as a comprehensive guide for anyone seeking to master the art of rapid relaxation and enhance their sleep quality.

Table of Contents

Chapter 1: Understanding the Need for Relaxation

The Impact of a Busy Lifestyle on Sleep

The modern lifestyle, characterized by relentless schedules and constant connectivity, significantly impacts our sleep quality and overall well-being. Busy individuals often find themselves juggling numerous responsibilities, from demanding jobs to family obligations, leaving little time for rest and relaxation. This perpetual busyness can lead to a cycle of sleep deprivation, where the urgency to complete tasks overshadows the essential need for adequate sleep. Understanding the nuances of how a busy lifestyle affects sleep is crucial for anyone seeking to improve their rest and rejuvenation.

One of the primary consequences of a hectic lifestyle is the tendency to prioritize work and social commitments over sleep. Many busy people adopt the mindset that sacrificing sleep is a necessary trade-off for productivity. This often results in late nights filled with work, scrolling through emails, or engaging in social media, which can disrupt natural sleep cycles. The blue light emitted by screens also interferes with the body's production of melatonin, the hormone responsible for regulating sleep. Consequently, individuals may struggle to fall asleep quickly, leading to a sense of fatigue that permeates their daily lives.

Moreover, the stress associated with a busy lifestyle can contribute to insomnia and other sleep disorders. When the mind is preoccupied with unresolved tasks or looming deadlines, it becomes increasingly difficult to unwind. This mental chatter can lead to anxiety, making it challenging to settle down for the night. Busy individuals may find themselves lying awake, replaying their to-do lists or worrying about future commitments, further exacerbating sleep troubles. Establishing a calming nighttime routine becomes essential for counteracting the stressors of the day and promoting a more restful night.

Physical health is also intricately linked to the quality of sleep, and a busy lifestyle often neglects this vital aspect. In the pursuit of efficiency, many busy people forgo exercise and healthy eating, both of which play a significant role in sleep quality. Sedentary behavior and poor dietary choices can lead to weight gain and other health issues, which can further disrupt sleep patterns. Engaging in regular physical activity and maintaining a balanced diet can enhance sleep quality, making it easier to fall asleep faster and stay asleep longer.

Finally, recognizing the importance of sleep is a critical step for busy individuals seeking to improve their overall health and productivity. Embracing the idea that adequate rest is not a luxury but a necessity can lead to transformative changes in lifestyle. Implementing simple strategies, such as setting consistent sleep schedules, creating a relaxing bedtime environment, and practicing mindfulness, can significantly enhance sleep quality. By prioritizing sleep amidst a busy lifestyle, individuals can achieve a more balanced life, where productivity and well-being coexist harmoniously

The Science of Relaxation

The Science of Relaxation delves into the physiological and psychological mechanisms that underlie the process of unwinding, particularly for those who find it challenging to transition from a relentless pace to a state of calm. In our fast-paced world, busy individuals often experience heightened stress levels, which can inhibit their ability to relax and subsequently fall asleep. Understanding the science behind relaxation is crucial for developing effective strategies that facilitate this transition, improving overall well-being and sleep quality.

At the core of relaxation lies the autonomic nervous system, which regulates bodily functions such as heart rate, digestion, and respiratory rate. It comprises two main branches: the sympathetic nervous system, responsible for the body's 'fight or flight' response, and the parasympathetic nervous system, which promotes 'rest and digest' activities. When busy people engage in activities that increase stress, such as tight deadlines or constant multitasking, the sympathetic system dominates, leading to elevated cortisol levels and heightened alertness. To combat this, techniques that stimulate the parasympathetic system, such as deep breathing and mindfulness, can be employed to restore balance and facilitate relaxation.

The role of breathing in relaxation cannot be overstated. Research has shown that controlled breathing techniques can significantly reduce stress and anxiety levels, promoting a sense of tranquility. Practices such as diaphragmatic breathing—where one breathes deeply into the abdomen rather than shallowly into the chest—activate the vagus nerve, which in turn stimulates the parasympathetic nervous system. For busy individuals, incorporating such breathing exercises into their daily routine can serve as a powerful tool for managing stress and enhancing relaxation, particularly before bedtime.

Mindfulness and meditation also play a crucial role in the science of relaxation. These practices encourage individuals to focus on the present moment, reducing the tendency to ruminate on past events or future worries, which can be significant barriers to relaxation and sleep. Studies indicate that regular mindfulness practice can lead to reductions in anxiety, improved mood, and better sleep outcomes. Busy people can benefit from integrating short, structured mindfulness sessions into their day, allowing them to cultivate a habit of relaxation that not only aids in winding down at night but also enhances their overall resilience to daily stressors.

Finally, the importance of creating a conducive environment for relaxation cannot be overlooked. Factors such as lighting, noise levels, and temperature can significantly impact one's ability to unwind. Research suggests that a cool, dark, and quiet space is optimal for promoting sleep. For busy individuals, making small adjustments—such as dimming lights an hour before bed or using white noise machines—can create an atmosphere that encourages relaxation. By understanding and applying the science of relaxation, busy people can develop effective strategies to enhance their ability to fall asleep faster and achieve a more restful night's sleep.

Recognizing Your Stress Triggers

Understanding your stress triggers is a crucial step in managing the overwhelming pressures of daily life. For busy individuals juggling multiple responsibilities, recognizing these triggers can significantly improve your ability to unwind and promote faster sleep. Stress often manifests in various forms, such as irritability, anxiety, or physical tension, and identifying the root causes can help you address them effectively. By learning to recognize your stress triggers, you can take proactive steps to mitigate their impact, paving the way for a more restful and rejuvenating sleep.

Begin by observing your daily routines and the patterns that emerge in your emotional and physical responses. Keep a stress journal for a week, noting moments when you feel overwhelmed, anxious, or unable to relax. Make sure to include the context of these feelings—what was happening at the time, who you were with, and any thoughts that crossed your mind. This exercise will encourage you to reflect on your experiences and identify recurring themes that may point to specific stressors.
Understanding these triggers lays the groundwork for developing strategies to cope with stress more effectively.

Common stress triggers for busy people often include work-related pressures, family obligations, or unexpected life changes. For instance, looming deadlines or heavy workloads can create a sense of urgency that heightens stress levels, making it difficult to transition into relaxation mode at the end of the day. Similarly, personal responsibilities such as childcare, household chores, or social commitments can contribute to feelings of overwhelm. By pinpointing these stressors, you can start to prioritize and delegate tasks, creating a more manageable schedule that allows for downtime and relaxation.

Environmental factors can also play a significant role in triggering stress. A cluttered workspace, loud noises, or even poor lighting can contribute to feelings of anxiety and restlessness. Recognizing these environmental influences is essential for creating a soothing atmosphere conducive to relaxation and better sleep. Make a conscious effort to declutter your space, incorporate calming colors, and introduce elements that promote tranquility, such as plants or soft lighting. By modifying your surroundings, you can diminish the impact of external stressors and create a more peaceful environment.

Lastly, remember that stress triggers can evolve over time. As life changes, so too may the factors that contribute to your stress levels. Regularly revisiting your stress journal and reflecting on your experiences will help you stay attuned to your emotional landscape. This ongoing self-awareness not only enables you to recognize new triggers but also reinforces your ability to implement effective relaxation tactics. By investing time in understanding your stress triggers, you empower yourself to reclaim your evenings and enhance the quality of your sleep, fostering a more balanced and peaceful life.

Chapter 2: The Psychology of Sleep

How Sleep Affects Productivity

Sleep plays a critical role in determining productivity levels, particularly for busy individuals juggling multiple responsibilities. The relationship between sleep and productivity is often underestimated, yet it is essential for optimal functioning. When we consider the demands of modern life—work deadlines, family obligations, and social commitments—it becomes clear that sleep is often sacrificed in the pursuit of efficiency. However, understanding how sleep affects productivity can inspire a shift in priorities, leading to improved performance in both professional and personal spheres.

Quality sleep is fundamental for cognitive functions such as memory, attention, and problem-solving. During sleep, the brain undergoes processes that consolidate memories and clear out toxins that accumulate throughout the day. A well-rested mind is better equipped to tackle complex tasks, make sound decisions, and engage in creative thinking. Conversely, inadequate sleep can lead to cognitive impairment, resulting in slower reaction times, diminished focus, and an increased likelihood of making mistakes. For busy individuals, this means that a few extra hours spent awake might yield diminishing returns on productivity, as fatigue can severely undermine one's ability to perform effectively.

Moreover, sleep influences emotional regulation, which is crucial for maintaining interpersonal relationships and navigating workplace dynamics. Lack of sleep can lead to irritability, heightened stress levels, and decreased patience. This emotional volatility not only affects personal well-being but also impacts interactions with colleagues, friends, and family. Busy people who neglect their sleep may find themselves more prone to conflicts and misunderstandings, which can further drain their energy and detract from their productivity. Recognizing the link between emotional health and sleep can motivate individuals to prioritize rest as a means of enhancing not just their work output, but also their overall quality of life.

In addition to cognitive and emotional aspects, sleep is also crucial for physical health, which directly correlates with productivity. Insufficient sleep has been linked to a range of health issues, including obesity, cardiovascular disease, and weakened immune function. When individuals do not get enough restorative sleep, they may experience fatigue and lethargy, making it difficult to maintain the energy levels needed for their daily tasks. In contrast, adequate sleep fosters a healthier lifestyle, leading to better physical stamina and resilience. For busy people, investing in sleep is not merely a personal health choice, it is a strategic move to enhance performance and sustain energy levels throughout the day.

To harness the benefits of sleep for improved productivity, busy individuals should adopt practical strategies for enhancing their sleep quality. Establishing a consistent sleep schedule, creating a calming bedtime routine, and optimizing the sleep environment can help facilitate faster and more restful sleep. Additionally, managing stress through relaxation techniques—such as mindfulness or deep breathing—can prepare the mind and body for restorative slumber. By recognizing sleep as a vital component of productivity, busy people can reclaim their time and energy, leading to greater success in both their professional and personal endeavors.

The Stages of Sleep

Sleep is a complex biological process that encompasses several stages, each playing a crucial role in the overall quality of rest and recovery. Understanding these stages can empower busy individuals to maximize their sleep efficiency and ultimately fall asleep faster. This knowledge becomes particularly beneficial for those whose hectic schedules often compromise their ability to recharge effectively.

The sleep cycle is primarily divided into two categories: Non-Rapid Eye Movement (NREM) sleep and Rapid Eye Movement (REM) sleep. NREM sleep is further segmented into three stages: N1, N2, and N3. The first stage, N1, marks the transition from wakefulness to sleep and typically lasts only a few minutes. During this phase, the body begins to relax, heart rate slows, and brain activity starts to decrease. Recognizing this stage can help busy individuals identify the onset of sleep, allowing them to create an environment conducive to falling asleep more quickly.

Stage N2 is where the majority of our sleep occurs, accounting for about 50% of the total sleep cycle. In this stage, body temperature drops, and heart rate continues to decrease. The brain produces sleep spindles and K-complexes, which are essential for memory consolidation and learning. For those with demanding schedules, maximizing time spent in Stage N2 can enhance cognitive function and overall productivity, ensuring that even short sleep periods yield significant restorative benefits.

Stage N3, also known as deep sleep, is the most restorative phase of NREM sleep. It is characterized by slow brain waves, and during this time, the body undergoes critical repair processes. Growth hormone is released, and tissue growth and muscle repair occur. Busy individuals often overlook the importance of deep sleep, yet it is during this stage that fatigue is alleviated, and energy levels are replenished. Creating routines that promote uninterrupted deep sleep can be particularly advantageous for those who need to wake up refreshed and ready to tackle demanding tasks.

Finally, REM sleep is crucial for emotional regulation and cognitive functioning. It typically occurs about 90 minutes after falling asleep and recurs throughout the night. During this stage, brain activity resembles that of wakefulness, and most vivid dreaming occurs. For busy people, REM sleep is essential for creative thinking, problem-solving, and emotional resilience. Prioritizing a consistent sleep schedule can enhance the likelihood of experiencing a full cycle of REM sleep, allowing for better emotional stability and sharper mental acuity. By understanding and optimizing these stages of sleep, individuals can cultivate strategies to fall asleep faster and improve their overall quality of life.

Myths and Misconceptions About Sleep

Myths and misconceptions about sleep abound, particularly among busy individuals who often prioritize work and productivity over rest. Many people believe that they can function well on minimal sleep, thinking that their bodies can adapt to these conditions. However, research has consistently shown that insufficient sleep can lead to a range of negative consequences, including impaired cognitive function, decreased productivity, and long-term health issues. It is essential to understand that sleep is not merely a luxury but a fundamental necessity for optimal performance and overall well-being.

One common myth is that napping is a sign of laziness. In reality, short naps can be an effective way to rejuvenate the mind and body, especially for those who may not be getting enough sleep at night. A power nap of 20 to 30 minutes can enhance alertness, improve mood, and boost cognitive performance. Busy individuals often overlook this simple strategy, believing that they must push through fatigue instead of taking a brief respite to recharge. Embracing napping as a legitimate tool for productivity can help redefine how we view rest.

Another misconception is that alcohol can aid sleep. While many people believe that a nightcap will help them fall asleep faster, the truth is that alcohol disrupts the sleep cycle. Although it may help one fall asleep initially, it often leads to fragmented sleep and a decrease in restorative REM cycles. Consequently, busy people who rely on alcohol for sleep may find themselves waking up feeling groggy and unfocused, undermining their efforts to stay productive during the day. Understanding the effects of alcohol on sleep is crucial for those seeking to improve their overall sleep quality.

Additionally, there is a widespread belief that one can "catch up" on sleep during the weekends after a busy workweek. This notion is misleading. While sleeping in might provide temporary relief, it does not compensate for the cumulative sleep deprivation experienced during the week. The body thrives on consistent sleep patterns, and erratic sleep schedules can disrupt the circadian rhythm, leading to further sleep difficulties.

Busy individuals should prioritize establishing a regular sleep routine to enhance their ability to fall asleep faster and reap the benefits of restorative sleep.

Finally, many busy people think that screen time before bed is harmless or even beneficial for winding down. However, the blue light emitted from screens can interfere with the production of melatonin, the hormone responsible for regulating sleep. This disruption can make it harder to fall asleep and negatively impact sleep quality. To improve sleep, it is advisable to establish a technology-free wind-down routine that promotes relaxation and prepares the mind and body for rest. By debunking these myths and misconceptions about sleep, busy individuals can take actionable steps toward achieving better rest and enhancing their overall productivity.

Chapter 3: Creating the Ideal Sleep Environment

The Importance of a Sleep-Friendly Room

Creating a sleep-friendly room is essential for busy individuals seeking to maximize their rest and recovery. The environment in which one sleeps significantly impacts the quality of sleep, which in turn affects overall health, productivity, and well-being. For those juggling demanding schedules, optimizing the bedroom can serve as a vital strategy to promote quicker sleep onset and deeper rest.

The first step in establishing a sleep-friendly room is controlling the light levels. Exposure to light, especially blue light from screens, can disrupt the body's natural circadian rhythms, making it harder to fall asleep. Investing in blackout curtains can help eliminate external light sources, creating a dark environment conducive to sleep. Additionally, utilizing dimmable lights or bedside lamps with warm hues can signal to the brain that it is time to wind down, fostering an atmosphere that encourages relaxation.

Temperature regulation plays a critical role in sleep quality. The ideal bedroom temperature for sleep is typically between 60 to 67 degrees Fahrenheit. This cooler environment allows the body to lower its core temperature, a natural process that occurs during sleep. For busy people who often experience stress and tension, a well-ventilated room with appropriate temperature control can help facilitate a quicker transition into sleep. Utilizing fans, air conditioning, or even breathable bedding can enhance comfort, making it easier to drift into slumber.

Minimizing noise is another essential aspect of creating a sleep-friendly room. For those living in bustling urban areas or busy households, disruptive sounds can significantly hinder the ability to fall asleep and stay asleep. Soundproofing techniques, such as using heavy curtains, rugs, and sound machines, can help create a serene environment.

Additionally, establishing a pre-sleep routine that includes calming activities can help signal to the mind that it is time to rest, further reducing the impact of external noises.

Finally, the organization and cleanliness of the sleep environment cannot be overlooked. A cluttered space can lead to increased stress and anxiety, making it difficult to unwind. Keeping the bedroom tidy, free of distractions, and reserved solely for rest can enhance the psychological association with sleep. By curating a designated sleep sanctuary, busy individuals can foster an atmosphere that not only supports rapid relaxation but also promotes overall well-being, ensuring they wake up refreshed and ready to tackle their demanding days.

Choosing the Right Bedding and Pillows

Choosing the right bedding and pillows is a crucial step in creating an environment conducive to rapid relaxation and restful sleep. For busy individuals, the quality of sleep significantly impacts productivity and overall well-being. The right bedding not only enhances comfort but also helps regulate body temperature, which is vital for falling asleep quickly and staying asleep throughout the night. This subchapter will explore key considerations for selecting bedding and pillows that support better sleep habits.

When it comes to sheets, material choice plays a significant role in comfort. Natural fibers, such as cotton and linen, are highly breathable and effective at regulating temperature, making them ideal for sleep. Cotton, particularly percale or sateen weaves, offers softness and durability, while linen is known for its moisture-wicking properties. For those who may sweat during the night, moisture-wicking fabrics can help keep you cool and comfortable, facilitating a quicker transition to sleep. Additionally, consider the thread count; while higher numbers can indicate softness, it is essential to balance this with breathability to avoid overheating.

Blankets and comforters also deserve careful consideration. opt for lightweight options that provide warmth without excessive weight, as heavy bedding can inhibit movement and lead to discomfort. Look for materials that offer insulation yet allow for airflow, such as down or down-alternative fills. These materials can help maintain an optimal body temperature, which is crucial for falling asleep faster. Additionally, choosing duvet covers and blankets in calming colors can create a soothing visual environment, further promoting relaxation.

Pillows are another essential aspect of creating a restful sleep environment. The right pillow should support the natural alignment of the spine, which varies depending on sleeping position. Side sleepers often benefit from firmer, loftier pillows that fill the gap between the head and shoulders, while back sleepers may prefer medium support to maintain neck alignment. Stomach sleepers typically require softer, flatter pillows to prevent strain on the neck. Memory foam and latex pillows can offer personalized support by contouring to the shape of the head and neck, ensuring comfort throughout the night.

Finally, maintaining cleanliness and freshness of bedding is vital for an optimal sleep environment. Regular washing of sheets, pillowcases, and duvet covers helps eliminate dust mites and allergens that can disrupt sleep. Additionally, consider using mattress protectors that can safeguard against spills and wear while providing an extra layer of comfort. By choosing the right bedding and pillows and maintaining a clean sleep environment, busy individuals can enhance their ability to fall asleep faster and enjoy the restorative sleep necessary for peak performance in their daily lives.

Managing Light and Noise

In the quest for rapid relaxation and improved sleep quality, managing light and noise in your environment is crucial. For busy individuals, external stimuli can significantly interfere with the ability to fall asleep quickly and achieve restorative rest. Understanding how these factors affect your sleep can empower you to create an optimal environment that promotes relaxation and enhances your overall well-being.

Light plays a pivotal role in regulating the body's circadian rhythm, which governs the sleep-wake cycle. Exposure to bright light, especially blue light emitted by screens, can signal to the brain that it is still daytime, making it difficult to wind down. To mitigate this, consider implementing a "digital sunset" by limiting screen time in the hours leading up to bedtime. Additionally, using blackout curtains or an eye mask can help create a dark sleeping environment that supports the production of melatonin, the hormone responsible for inducing sleep.

Noise, much like light, can disrupt the peacefulness needed for a good night's rest. Busy lifestyles often expose individuals to a variety of sounds, from traffic to household activities. To counteract this, soundproofing your bedroom can be beneficial. Simple solutions include using heavy curtains, rugs, or even soundproof panels to absorb unwanted noise. Moreover, introducing white noise machines or soothing sound apps can mask disruptive sounds, creating a calming backdrop that promotes relaxation and helps you fall asleep faster.

Creating a sleep-conducive environment requires a holistic approach that considers both light and noise. It is essential to establish a pre-sleep routine that signals to your body that it is time to unwind. Dim the lights an hour before bed, engage in relaxing activities, and ensure your sleeping area is quiet and comfortable. By making these adjustments, you can create a sanctuary that encourages deep relaxation and prepares you for restorative sleep, even amidst a busy lifestyle.

Ultimately, managing light and noise is about taking control of your environment. By being proactive in reducing these distractions, busy individuals can significantly enhance their ability to fall asleep faster and enjoy a more restful night. Slight changes, such as adjusting lighting and utilizing sound-masking techniques, can lead to substantial improvements in sleep quality. As you incorporate these strategies into your routine, you will find that relaxation becomes more attainable, allowing you to wake up refreshed and ready to tackle the demands of your day.

Chapter 4: Daily Habits for Better Sleep

The Role of Diet in Sleep Quality

The connection between diet and sleep quality is often overlooked in the busy lives of many individuals. As the pace of life accelerates, people may find themselves reaching for quick, often unhealthy, meals that can impact their ability to relax and fall asleep efficiently. Understanding the role of diet in sleep quality is vital for busy people seeking to enhance their nightly rest and overall well-being.

First, the timing of meals plays a crucial role in sleep patterns. Eating large meals close to bedtime can lead to discomfort and indigestion, making it challenging to drift off into a restful sleep. It is recommended to have the last meal of the day at least two to three hours before going to bed. This allows the body adequate time to digest food, reducing the likelihood of sleep disturbances. For those with hectic schedules, planning meals in advance can help mitigate the temptation to indulge in late-night snacking, which often consists of sugary or fatty foods that can disrupt sleep.

The quality of food consumed also significantly influences sleep. Diets high in refined carbohydrates, sugars, and unhealthy fats can lead to fluctuations in blood sugar levels, affecting energy and mood throughout the day. In contrast, a balanced diet rich in whole foods, such as fruits, vegetables, whole grains, lean proteins, and healthy fats, promotes stable energy levels and can enhance sleep quality. Nutrients like magnesium and tryptophan, found in foods such as nuts, seeds, and turkey, are known to facilitate relaxation and support the production of melatonin, the hormone responsible for regulating sleep.

Caffeine and alcohol are two major dietary components that can severely impact sleep quality. Caffeine, commonly found in coffee, tea, and many energy drinks, is a stimulant that can stay in the system for hours, making it difficult to fall asleep if consumed too late in the day. On the other hand, while alcohol may initially seem to promote relaxation, it can disrupt the sleep cycle and lead to fragmented sleep. Busy individuals should be mindful of their intake of these substances, particularly in the hours leading up to bedtime, to optimize their chances of falling asleep quickly and enjoying a restorative night's rest.

Finally, hydration also plays a role in sleep quality. While staying hydrated is essential for overall health, excessive fluid intake right before bed can lead to frequent trips to the bathroom, interrupting sleep. It is advisable to drink plenty of water throughout the day while tapering off fluid consumption as bedtime approaches. By being mindful of dietary habits, busy people can create a more conducive environment for sleep, leading to improved relaxation, better energy levels, and enhanced productivity during waking hours.

Exercise and it's Sleep Benefits

Exercise is a powerful tool that can significantly enhance the quality of sleep, a benefit often overlooked by busy individuals juggling multiple responsibilities. Engaging in regular physical activity not only helps to reduce stress and anxiety but also promotes a more efficient sleep cycle. For those frequently battling fatigue and restlessness, incorporating exercise into daily routines can pave the way for faster and more restful sleep. This subchapter will explore the relationship between exercise and sleep, highlighting how even small adjustments can lead to remarkable changes.

Research indicates that engaging in moderate aerobic exercise can help individuals fall asleep faster and enjoy deeper sleep. The physiological effects of exercise, such as increased body temperature and the subsequent cooling down process, signal the body that it is time to rest. This natural process can help regulate the circadian rhythm, making it easier to fall asleep at night. For busy people, integrating even short bursts of physical activity can lead to improved sleep patterns. Aim for at least 30 minutes of moderate exercise most days of the week, whether it is a brisk walk, a quick run, or a workout at the gym.

Moreover, exercise can serve as a powerful stress reliever, addressing one of the primary barriers to quality sleep. The demands of a busy lifestyle often lead to heightened stress levels, making it difficult for the mind to relax at night. Physical activity stimulates the production of endorphins, the body's natural mood lifters, which can alleviate feelings of anxiety and promote a sense of calm. By reducing stress through regular exercise, busy individuals may find it easier to unwind and prepare for sleep, leading to more restorative rest.

The timing of exercise also plays a crucial role in its effectiveness for sleep improvement. While some people may thrive on morning workouts, others may find that exercising in the late afternoon or early evening helps them wind down after a hectic day. It is essential for busy people to experiment with various times to find what best suits their schedules and sleep patterns. However, it is generally advisable to avoid vigorous exercise close to bedtime, as it may have a stimulating effect and delay the onset of sleep.

Incorporating exercise into a busy lifestyle does not have to be daunting. Simple changes, such as taking the stairs instead of the elevator, going for a walk during lunch breaks, or engaging in a quick home workout, can make a significant difference. By making physical activity a priority, busy individuals can not only enhance their overall well-being but also improve their sleep quality. As the journey toward better sleep begins, recognizing the powerful connection between exercise and rest is a vital step for anyone looking to recharge and rejuvenate in today's fast-paced world.

The Impact of Screen Time

In today's modern world, screens have become an integral part of our daily lives, influencing everything from how we work to how we relax. Busy individuals often find themselves glued to their devices for extended periods, whether it is for professional tasks, social interactions, or entertainment. While technology provides numerous conveniences, excessive screen time can lead to detrimental effects on both mental and physical health, particularly when it comes to achieving restful sleep. Understanding these impacts is crucial for anyone looking to optimize their relaxation and sleep quality.

One of the primary concerns associated with excessive screen time is its effect on the body's natural circadian rhythms. The blue light emitted by screens interferes with the production of melatonin, the hormone responsible for regulating sleep-wake cycles.
When busy individuals engage with their devices, especially in the hours leading up to bedtime, they inadvertently signal their brains to remain alert. This disruption can make
it significantly harder to fall asleep, resulting in a cascade of negative consequences, such as fatigue, irritability, and decreased productivity during the day.

Moreover, the content consumed during screen time can also play a role in sleep quality. Engaging with stimulating content—be it thrilling TV shows, intense video games, or even stressful work emails—can elevate heart rates and keep the mind racing. For busy people, who often juggle multiple responsibilities, this mental stimulation can carry over into the night, making it challenging to unwind. Establishing a calming pre-sleep routine that minimizes screen exposure can help create a more conducive environment for relaxation and sleep.

In addition to impacting sleep, prolonged screen time has been linked to various physical health issues, including eye strain and musculoskeletal problems. Busy individuals who spend hours hunched over devices may experience discomfort, which can further hinder their ability to relax and fall asleep. Incorporating regular breaks and practicing good ergonomics can mitigate these physical effects, allowing for a more comfortable experience that contributes to overall well-being.

Finally, it is essential to recognize the role of mindfulness in managing screen time. Busy people can benefit from setting boundaries around device usage, particularly in the evening hours. By prioritizing activities that promote relaxation—such as reading, meditating, or engaging in light stretching—individuals can create a buffer between their day-to-day stresses and the need for restful sleep. By taking conscious steps to reduce screen time, busy individuals can reclaim their evenings and pave the way for a more restful night's sleep, leading to improved performance and overall quality of life.

Chapter 5: Relaxation Techniques for Busy Lives

Breathing Exercises for Quick Calm

Breathing exercises are among the simplest yet most effective tools for achieving rapid relaxation, especially for busy individuals who often find themselves overwhelmed by the demands of daily life. The practice of controlled breathing can serve as a powerful antidote to stress, promoting a sense of calm that can help you fall asleep faster and improve your overall well-being. This subchapter will explore various breathing techniques designed to fit seamlessly into your hectic schedule, allowing you to take a moment to recharge and restore your mental clarity.

One of the most accessible breathing exercises is the 4-7-8 technique, which can be performed anywhere, anytime. To practice this method, begin by sitting or lying down in a comfortable position. Inhale deeply through your nose for a count of four, allowing your abdomen to rise as you fill your lungs with air. Hold your breath for a count of seven, during which you can visualize the stress leaving your body. Finally, exhale slowly through your mouth for a count of eight. This rhythmic cycle not only helps lower your heart rate but also activates your body's relaxation response, making it easier to transition into a restful state.

Another effective technique is diaphragmatic breathing, which focuses on engaging the diaphragm rather than shallow chest breathing. To practice this, place one hand on your chest and the other on your abdomen. Inhale deeply through your nose, ensuring your abdomen expands while your chest remains relatively still. This deep breathing pattern increases oxygen intake and promotes relaxation by stimulating the vagus nerve, which plays a crucial role in regulating stress. Incorporating diaphragmatic breathing into your evening routine can create a peaceful environment conducive to sleep.

For those moments when you need to unwind rapidly, the box breathing technique offers a structured approach to calming the mind. This method involves inhaling, holding, exhaling, and holding again for equal counts—typically four seconds each. Start by inhaling through your nose for four seconds, holding your breath for another four seconds, and then exhaling through your mouth for four seconds. After the exhale, hold your breath for a final four seconds before starting the cycle again. This exercise not only helps ground your thoughts but also enhances focus, making it an excellent choice for busy individuals looking to quiet their minds before bedtime.

Incorporating these breathing exercises into your daily routine can yield significant benefits for your mental and emotional health. Even a few minutes of focused breathing can disrupt negative thought patterns and create a sense of tranquility that permeates your entire being. By committing to regular practice, you can train your body to respond to stressors with calmness, leading to easier transitions into sleep and improved overall relaxation. Taking the time to practice these techniques can transform your approach to stress management, allowing you to power down and embrace a more restful night's sleep.

Guided Imagery and Visualization

Guided imagery and visualization are powerful techniques that can significantly enhance your ability to relax and fall asleep faster, especially for busy individuals who often find their minds racing at the end of the day. These methods involve creating mental images and scenarios that promote a sense of calm and tranquility, effectively allowing your busy brain to disengage from the stresses of daily life. By focusing your mind on peaceful and soothing imagery, you can facilitate a smoother transition into sleep, making it easier to leave the day's worries behind.

The essence of guided imagery lies in its ability to engage the senses. When practicing this technique, you are encouraged to visualize specific scenes that evoke feelings of relaxation. It could be a serene beach, a tranquil forest, or a cozy cabin in the mountains. By immersing yourself in these mental images, you can tap into the calming sensations associated with them—such as the sound of waves, the rustling of leaves, or the warmth of a fire. This sensory engagement not only distracts you from intrusive thoughts but also signals to your body that it is time to unwind, paving the way for a restful night's sleep.

For busy individuals, the practice of visualization can be easily integrated into a nightly routine. Setting aside just a few minutes before bed to engage in guided imagery can create a significant impact on your ability to fall asleep. Begin by finding a comfortable position, closing your eyes, and taking several deep breaths. As you breathe in and out, picture your chosen scene in vivid detail. Imagine the colors, sounds, and even scents associated with it. By fully immersing yourself in this mental exercise, you can create a mental sanctuary that promotes relaxation and prepares your mind for sleep.

Incorporating guided imagery into your daily routine can also serve as a beneficial tool during particularly stressful periods. Busy schedules often lead to an accumulation of tension, making it difficult for the mind to quiet down at night. Utilizing visualization techniques during the day—whether during a break, while commuting, or before a meeting—can help mitigate stress levels and provide a mental reset. This practice not only aids in immediate relaxation but also helps reinforce a habit of calmness that can carry into your evening routine, ultimately leading to improved sleep quality.

Lastly, the benefits of guided imagery extend beyond just falling asleep faster. Engaging in this practice can enhance overall well-being by promoting mindfulness and reducing anxiety. As busy individuals learn to harness the power of their imagination, they cultivate a greater sense of control over their thoughts and emotions. By regularly practicing guided imagery, you can develop a healthier relationship with stress and sleep, enabling you to recharge more effectively and face each day with renewed energy and focus.

Progressive Muscle Relaxation

Progressive Muscle Relaxation (PMR) is a powerful technique designed to help individuals unwind and release tension from their bodies. It involves systematically tensing and then relaxing various muscle groups, promoting a deep sense of relaxation. As busy people often find themselves overwhelmed with stress and mental fatigue, PMR offers a practical solution to combat these challenges. By incorporating this technique into your evening routine, you can significantly enhance your ability to fall asleep faster and achieve a more restorative rest.

The process of PMR begins with an awareness of bodily sensations. It encourages you to focus on the difference between tension and relaxation. By taking a moment to close your eyes and breathe deeply, you can center your thoughts and prepare your mind for the exercise. Begin with your feet, tensing the muscles for a count of five before releasing the tension and feeling the relaxation wash over you. Gradually move up through your body—calves, thighs, abdomen, arms, and face—allowing yourself to experience the distinct contrast between tension and relaxation in each area.

One of the key benefits of PMR is its ability to reduce anxiety and promote mental calmness. In the hustle and bustle of daily life, it is easy to carry stress in your muscles without even realizing it. This technique encourages you to consciously release that built-up tension, facilitating a deeper state of relaxation that can help quiet racing thoughts. By practicing PMR regularly, individuals can develop a greater awareness of their body and the stressors they carry, leading to a more peaceful mindset conducive to sleep.

In addition to its mental benefits, PMR can also have a positive impact on physical health. Chronic muscle tension is often linked to a variety of issues, including headaches, digestive problems, and sleep disturbances. By integrating PMR into your nighttime ritual, you can alleviate these physical symptoms and promote overall well-being. As muscles relax, blood flow increases, and the body can shift into a state of recovery, making it easier to transition into sleep.

To get started with PMR, it is advisable to set aside a specific time each night. Find a quiet, comfortable space free from distractions, and allocate 10 to 20 minutes for the exercise.
As you become more familiar with the technique, you may find it easier to incorporate PMR into your day, using it as a tool to manage stress in real-time. By committing to this practice, you not only enhance your ability to fall asleep faster but also cultivate a healthier relationship with your body and mind, paving the way for more peaceful nights and energized days.

Chapter 6: Mindfulness and Meditation

Understanding Mindfulness

Mindfulness is a practice rooted in ancient traditions, yet it holds profound relevance in today's fast-paced world, particularly for busy individuals seeking to unwind and recharge. At its core, mindfulness involves paying deliberate attention to the present moment without judgment. This simple yet powerful practice can help busy people cultivate a sense of awareness that can be particularly beneficial for those struggling to fall asleep. By training the mind to focus on the here and now, individuals can alleviate stress and create a more conducive environment for relaxation and rest.

In a world filled with distractions, the ability to be present is often compromised. Our minds tend to race with thoughts about unfinished tasks, deadlines, and obligations, making it difficult to achieve a state of calm. Mindfulness counters this tendency by encouraging practitioners to observe their thoughts and feelings as they arise, acknowledging them without getting caught up in the narrative. This practice of observing rather than reacting allows for a greater sense of control over one's mental landscape, paving the way for improved sleep by reducing the mental clutter that can keep one awake at night.

Furthermore, mindfulness fosters a deeper connection with the body, which is essential for relaxation. Busy people often neglect their physical sensations, leading to a disconnect that can exacerbate stress. By engaging in mindfulness, individuals can tune into their bodies, recognizing tension and discomfort that may have gone unnoticed.
This heightened awareness can prompt simple yet effective relaxation techniques, such as deep breathing or gentle stretching, which can significantly ease the transition to sleep. As the body relaxes, so too does the mind, creating a harmonious state that is conducive to falling asleep faster.

Incorporating mindfulness into one's daily routine does not require extensive time commitments. Even a few minutes of mindful practice each day can yield significant benefits. Techniques such as mindful breathing, where one focuses solely on the rhythm of their breath, or body scans, which involve mentally checking in with various parts of the body, can be easily integrated into a busy schedule. These practices can serve as powerful tools to help individuals wind down at the end of the day, signaling to the body that it is time to rest and prepare for sleep.

Ultimately, understanding mindfulness is about recognizing its potential to transform the way busy people approach relaxation and sleep. By cultivating a mindful mindset,
individuals can break the cycle of stress and restlessness that often accompanies a hectic lifestyle. Embracing mindfulness not only enhances one's ability to fall asleep faster but also enriches overall well-being, leading to a more balanced and fulfilling life. As busy individuals learn to harness the power of mindfulness, they can find solace in the present moment and create the mental space necessary for rejuvenation and restful sleep.

Simple Meditation Techniques

Meditation can seem daunting, especially for those with busy schedules, but simple techniques can make it accessible and effective for anyone looking to unwind and fall asleep faster. The core of meditation is about finding stillness amidst the chaos of daily life, and even a few minutes of practice can significantly improve your ability to relax. This subchapter will guide you through straightforward meditation techniques that can seamlessly fit into your routine, helping you cultivate a sense of calm and prepare your mind for sleep.

One of the simplest techniques is focused breathing. This method involves paying close attention to your breath as it flows in and out of your body. To begin, find a comfortable position, either seated or lying down. Close your eyes, and take a deep breath in through your nose, allowing your abdomen to expand. Hold it for a moment, then exhale slowly through your mouth. Aim to count each breath, inhaling for four counts, holding for four, and exhaling for six. This structured rhythm not only calms the mind but also signals your body that it is time to relax, making it easier to transition into sleep.

Another effective technique is a body scan meditation. This practice encourages you to connect with your body and release tension. Start by lying down in a comfortable position. Close your eyes and take a few deep breaths. Then, begin to mentally "scan" your body from head to toe, paying attention to any areas of tightness or discomfort. As you focus on each part, consciously relax those muscles, allowing a sense of heaviness to wash over you. This technique not only promotes relaxation but also heightens your awareness of bodily sensations, fostering a deeper connection to yourself that can be particularly beneficial before sleep.

Visualization is another powerful method to ease the mind. This technique involves creating a mental image that brings you peace and tranquility. Picture a serene location, such as a quiet beach or a lush forest. As you breathe deeply, immerse yourself in the details of this place: the sound of waves, the smell of pine, or the warmth of the sun.

Engaging all your senses in this visualization helps distract your mind from the stresses of the day and can create a calming environment conducive to sleep. By anchoring your thoughts to this peaceful scene, you can gently guide yourself into a more restful state.

Lastly, consider incorporating loving-kindness meditation into your routine. This technique is particularly beneficial for busy people who may experience stress or anxiety. It involves silently repeating phrases that express goodwill and compassion towards yourself and others. Begin by focusing on yourself, repeating phrases like "May I be happy, may I be healthy, may I be at peace." Gradually extend these wishes to loved ones, acquaintances, and even those with whom you may have conflicts. This practice fosters a sense of connection and positivity, helping to alleviate negative thoughts that can hinder your ability to relax and fall asleep.

Incorporating these simple meditation techniques into your evening routine can transform your nighttime experience. By dedicating just a few minutes to focused breathing, body scanning, visualization, or loving-kindness meditation, you can create a peaceful transition from your busy day to a restful night. These practices not only promote relaxation but also empower you to cultivate mindfulness, enhancing your overall well-being and sleep quality. Embracing these techniques can lead to a more restful night, allowing you to wake up refreshed and ready to tackle the challenges of a new day.

Incorporating Mindfulness into Daily Routine

Incorporating mindfulness into daily routines can significantly enhance your ability to relax and fall asleep faster, particularly for busy individuals who often struggle to unwind at the end of a hectic day. Mindfulness is not just a trend; it is a practice rooted in ancient traditions that promotes awareness of the present moment. By integrating simple mindfulness techniques into your daily life, you can cultivate a greater sense of calm and reduce the mental clutter that often hinders restful sleep.

One of the easiest ways to incorporate mindfulness is through intentional breathing exercises. Taking just a few moments throughout the day to focus on your breath can create a profound shift in your mental state. When you feel overwhelmed, pause, and take a few deep breaths. Inhale deeply through your nose, allowing your abdomen to expand, and then exhale slowly through your mouth. This practice can help ground you in the present moment and alleviate stress, making it easier to transition into a more relaxed state as bedtime approaches.

Another effective method is to practice mindfulness during routine activities. Whether you are eating lunch, commuting, or even washing dishes, try to engage fully in the experience. For instance, during meals, take the time to savor each bite, noticing the flavors and textures of the food. By bringing your attention to these simple tasks, you can train your mind to focus on the here and now rather than the endless to-do lists that often plague busy individuals. This shift in focus can help reduce anxiety and create a more peaceful mindset, paving the way for better sleep.

Establishing a mindful evening routine can also be beneficial in preparing your mind and body for rest. Consider setting aside 10 to 15 minutes before bed for a relaxation practice that includes gentle stretching or meditation. Use this time to reflect on your day, acknowledging any stressors without judgment. Engaging in a calming activity, such as reading a book or listening to soothing music, can further enhance your relaxation and signal to your body that it is time to wind down. Consistency with this routine can signal to your brain that it is time to transition from a busy day to a restful night.

Finally, technology can play a role in fostering mindfulness by offering tools that remind you to take breaks and practice relaxation techniques. Consider using apps that promote mindfulness through guided meditations or reminders for mindful breathing. These digital resources can serve as gentle nudges to pause and reconnect with yourself amidst a busy schedule. By intentionally incorporating mindfulness into your daily life, you create a powerful counterbalance to the demands of a fast-paced lifestyle, ultimately leading to quicker and more restful sleep.

Chapter 7: Power Naps and Their Benefits

The Science Behind Napping

Napping has long been regarded as a luxury or an indulgence, often associated with leisure rather than productivity. However, recent research underscores the science behind napping and its significant benefits for busy individuals seeking rapid relaxation and improved performance. Understanding the physiological and psychological effects of napping can empower you to embrace this practice as an essential tool in your busy lifestyle.

The primary mechanism through which napping influences our body is sleep architecture. A typical sleep cycle includes distinct stages, with rapid eye movement (REM) and non-REM sleep playing crucial roles in cognitive function and memory consolidation. Naps can be strategically timed to tap into these stages, allowing for enhanced alertness and quicker recovery from fatigue. Studies suggest that even short naps—around 10 to 20 minutes—can help you achieve a light stage of non-REM sleep, which refreshes the mind without causing grogginess.

Moreover, the duration of a nap can determine its effectiveness. A brief nap of about 20 minutes can significantly enhance alertness and cognitive performance, making it ideal for busy professionals needing a quick boost. On the other hand, longer naps of 60 to 90 minutes can allow for a full sleep cycle, including REM sleep, which is critical for creative thinking and problem-solving. Understanding your personal needs and experimenting with different nap lengths can enable you to harness the full potential of napping in your day-to-day routine.

The benefits of napping extend beyond mere alertness; they also play a vital role in emotional regulation. A busy person often juggles multiple responsibilities, leading to stress and anxiety. Research indicates that napping can help reduce feelings of tension and improve mood. By giving your mind a chance to reset, you can approach challenges with a clearer perspective and increased resilience. This emotional boost can be particularly beneficial during high-pressure periods, allowing you to maintain focus and productivity.

Incorporating napping into your daily schedule does not have to be complicated. Finding a quiet space and setting aside just a few minutes during your day can yield significant benefits. Whether you choose to take a power nap during your lunch break or set an alarm for a quick recharge, the science supports the idea that napping is not only a feasible solution for busy people but also a smart strategy for maximizing efficiency and well-being. Embracing the science of napping can transform your approach to relaxation, making it an indispensable part of your busy life.

How to Nap Effectively

Napping can be an invaluable tool for busy individuals seeking to recharge their energy and enhance productivity. However, not all naps are created equal. To nap effectively, it is essential to understand the science behind sleep cycles, the optimal duration for a power nap, and the best practices for creating an environment conducive to relaxation. By mastering the art of napping, even the busiest professionals can find a few precious moments to rejuvenate their minds and bodies.

The first step to an effective nap is timing. Most adults experience a natural dip in energy levels during the early afternoon, typically between 1 p.m. and 3 p.m. This period is often marked by a decrease in alertness and productivity, making it an ideal time for a short nap. Aim for a duration of 10 to 20 minutes, as this timeframe allows you to enter the lighter stages of non-REM sleep without falling into deeper sleep, which can lead to grogginess upon waking. This short nap can significantly boost alertness and cognitive performance, making it a valuable strategy for busy professionals.

Creating the right environment for napping is essential for effectiveness. Choose a quiet, dimly lit space where you will not be disturbed. If you are in a public setting or an office, consider using an eye mask or noise-canceling headphones to block out distractions. The ideal temperature for napping is slightly cooler than normal room temperature, as this promotes relaxation. Additionally, consider using a comfortable pillow or blanket to make your resting space more inviting. By optimizing your environment, you set the stage for a more restful and rejuvenating nap.

Establishing a napping routine can further enhance the benefits of this practice. Consistency is key; try to nap at the same time each day to train your body to recognize when it is time to rest. This regularity helps reinforce your body's natural circadian rhythms and can make falling asleep faster easier. Also, listen to your body's signals. If you find yourself needing a nap more frequently or at different times, adjust your routine accordingly. A flexible approach to napping can help you maximize its benefits while accommodating your busy schedule.

Finally, be mindful of how napping fits into your overall sleep strategy. While napping can be a powerful tool for boosting energy and focus, it should not replace a good night's sleep. Ensure you are still prioritizing sufficient nighttime rest to maintain your overall health and well-being. Use naps as a supplement to your regular sleep schedule, rather than a substitute. By integrating effective napping into your daily routine, you empower yourself to tackle your busy life with renewed vigor and clarity.

Timing Your Naps for Maximum Benefit

Napping can be a powerful tool for busy individuals seeking to recharge their energy and improve productivity. However, the timing of your naps plays a crucial role in maximizing their benefits. Understanding the science behind sleep cycles can help you determine the most effective nap duration and timing to enhance your alertness and overall well- being. This subchapter delves into the optimal timing for naps to help you feel refreshed and ready to tackle your responsibilities.

The human sleep cycle typically consists of several stages, including light sleep, deep sleep, and REM (rapid eye movement) sleep. A full sleep cycle lasts approximately 90 minutes, but for quick rejuvenation, a short nap of 20 to 30 minutes can be highly effective. This duration allows you to enter the lighter stages of sleep without delving too deeply, minimizing grogginess upon waking. Busy individuals should aim to schedule their naps during the early afternoon when the body's natural circadian rhythm experiences a dip in alertness, making it an ideal time for a restorative break.

For those who find it challenging to fall asleep quickly, creating a conducive napping environment can make a significant difference. Limiting distractions, dimming the lights, and using sleep masks or earplugs can help signal to your body that it is time to rest.
Additionally, engaging in relaxation techniques, such as deep breathing or progressive muscle relaxation, can speed up falling asleep. Being intentional about your napping space and routine will enhance your ability to drift off quickly and enjoy the benefits of a well-timed nap.

While the early afternoon is generally the optimal time for a nap, individual variations in sleep needs and lifestyles must be considered. Some people may benefit from a brief mid-morning or late afternoon nap, especially if they experience fatigue at those times. Monitoring your energy levels throughout the day can help you identify when you feel the most tired. By tailoring your napping schedule to your personal rhythm, you can maximize the restorative effects of your naps and improve your overall productivity.

In conclusion, timing your naps strategically can significantly impact their effectiveness and your ability to power down amidst a busy schedule. By understanding your body's natural sleep patterns, creating a conducive environment, and personalizing your napping schedule, you can harness the benefits of napping to enhance alertness, productivity, and overall well-being. Embracing the power of a well-timed nap can be a game-changer for busy individuals striving to maintain peak performance in their daily lives.

Chapter 8: Establishing a Sleep Routine

The Importance of Consistency

In the realm of relaxation techniques, consistency plays a pivotal role in enhancing the effectiveness of practices aimed at helping busy individuals fall asleep faster. This principle is particularly crucial for those who juggle multiple responsibilities, as their schedules often leave little room for error when it comes to establishing a calming bedtime routine. Consistency not only reinforces the habit of relaxation but also signals to the body that it is time to unwind, thereby facilitating a smoother transition from the hustle and bustle of daily life to the tranquility of sleep.

When busy individuals commit to a regular relaxation schedule, they begin to create a mental association between specific activities and the onset of sleep. This could include practices such as meditation, deep breathing exercises, or gentle stretching. By engaging in these activities at the same time each evening, the body's internal clock, or circadian rhythm, becomes attuned to this ritual. As a result, the brain starts to recognize cues that indicate it is time to prepare for rest, making it easier to drift off into slumber when bedtime arrives.

Moreover, consistency can significantly decrease the time it takes to fall asleep. Research indicates that irregular sleep patterns can disrupt the body's natural hormone cycles, particularly the production of melatonin, which is essential for regulating sleep. By establishing a consistent routine that incorporates relaxation techniques, busy individuals can help stabilize these hormonal fluctuations. This stabilization not only promotes faster sleep onset but also enhances the overall quality of sleep, which is often compromised by the stress and demands of a busy lifestyle.

In addition to aiding in sleep onset, a consistent relaxation routine can act as a buffer against the cumulative stress that many busy people experience. When relaxation becomes a non-negotiable part of the daily routine, it serves as a protective mechanism that counters the toll of stress over time. This proactive approach allows individuals to manage their stress levels more effectively, leading to improved mental clarity and emotional resilience during the day. Consequently, they are better equipped to handle the challenges that come with their packed schedules.

Finally, the act of prioritizing consistency in relaxation practices fosters a greater sense of self-care and personal well-being. For busy individuals, life often revolves around obligations to others, leaving little room for personal time. By committing to a consistent relaxation routine, they reclaim a portion of their day dedicated solely to themselves. This shift not only nourishes their mental health but also reinforces the understanding that they deserve moments of peace, ultimately leading to a more balanced and fulfilling life. Consistency in relaxation is not just a strategy for falling asleep faster; it is a crucial element in nurturing overall well-being amidst the demands of a busy life.

Crafting Your Pre-Sleep Ritual

Creating an effective pre-sleep ritual is essential for busy individuals seeking to unwind and prepare their minds and bodies for restorative rest. In a world filled with constant stimulation and demanding schedules, establishing a calming routine can significantly enhance your ability to fall asleep faster and improve overall sleep quality. A well-crafted pre-sleep ritual sets the stage for relaxation, signaling to your body that it is time to transition from the hustle and bustle of the day to a peaceful night's rest.

The first step in crafting your pre-sleep ritual is to establish a consistent time for winding down each evening. This consistency helps regulate your body's internal clock, making it easier to fall asleep and wake up at the same time daily. Aim to begin your ritual about 30 to 60 minutes before your intended bedtime. This dedicated time should be free from distractions, allowing you to focus on activities that promote relaxation and calmness. By treating this period as sacred, you signal to your mind that it is time to shift gears and prioritize self-care.

Incorporating calming activities into your pre-sleep ritual is crucial. Consider practices such as gentle stretching, meditation, or reading a physical book. These activities can help lower your heart rate and reduce stress levels, making it easier to drift off to sleep. Avoid stimulating activities like checking emails, engaging in heated discussions, or watching thrilling movies, as these can elevate your adrenaline levels and hinder your ability to relax. Instead, opt for soothing music or nature sounds to create an environment conducive to sleep.

Another effective component of your pre-sleep ritual is the creation of a comfortable sleep environment. Pay attention to your bedroom's ambiance; ensure that it is dark, quiet, and cool. Consider using blackout curtains, white noise machines, or aromatherapy to enhance your space. The use of calming scents, such as lavender or chamomile, can signal to your brain that it is time to wind down. Additionally, invest in a comfortable mattress and pillows to support restful sleep. A tranquil environment complements your pre-sleep activities, reinforcing the relaxation process.

Finally, be mindful of your diet and the consumption of stimulants in the hours leading up to bedtime. Avoid large meals, caffeine, and alcohol close to your sleep time, as these can disrupt your ability to fall asleep. Instead, consider a light snack if you are hungry, such as a banana or a handful of nuts, which can support relaxation without overwhelming your digestive system. By aligning your dietary choices with your pre-sleep ritual, you create a holistic approach to falling asleep faster, enhancing the effectiveness of your nightly routine. In doing so, you empower yourself to reclaim your rest and rejuvenate your busy life.

Adjusting Your Routine for Changing Schedules

Adjusting your routine for changing schedules is crucial for busy individuals seeking to optimize their relaxation and sleep quality. As life's demands fluctuate—whether due to work commitments, family obligations, or unexpected events—our routines often need to adapt accordingly. Recognizing the importance of a flexible schedule can make a significant difference in how quickly and easily you fall asleep, enhancing both your productivity and overall well-being.

To effectively modify your routine, start by assessing your current schedule. Identify the specific areas that require adjustment, such as your bedtime, wake-up time, or pre-sleep activities. Consider how your obligations impact your ability to unwind. For instance, if you typically engage in a calming activity before sleep but find yourself with less time due to new responsibilities, it may be necessary to shorten the duration or change the timing of these activities. Prioritizing relaxation can help mitigate the effects of a hectic schedule on your sleep.

Creating a flexible yet structured framework for your daily routine is essential. Establish core activities that remain constant, such as meal times or essential work tasks, while allowing for variability in other areas. For example, if your work hours shift, try to maintain a consistent bedtime that aligns with your new wake-up time. This consistency can signal to your body when it is time to wind down, making it easier to transition into sleep despite the changes in your daily life.

Incorporating relaxation techniques into your adjusted routine can further enhance your ability to fall asleep quickly. Techniques such as deep breathing exercises, progressive muscle relaxation, or mindful meditation can be easily integrated into your evening rituals, regardless of how your day unfolds. Even just a few minutes dedicated to these practices can significantly lower stress levels and prepare your mind for rest. Experiment with different methods to find what resonates best with you, ensuring that your routine remains effective no matter the circumstances.

Finally, it is important to remain adaptable and patient with yourself as you navigate these changes. Life is inherently unpredictable, and your ability to adjust your routine will be tested from time to time. Listen to your body and recognize when you need to modify your approach further. Keeping a sleep journal can help you track how changes in your routine impact your sleep quality, enabling you to refine your strategies for falling asleep faster as your schedule evolves. Embracing this flexibility will empower you to maintain a sense of calm and control, even amidst the chaos of a busy life.

Chapter 9: Overcoming Sleep Challenges

Identifying Common Sleep Disorders

Identifying common sleep disorders is crucial for busy individuals struggling to fall asleep quickly and effectively. In our fast-paced lives, understanding the barriers to restful sleep can empower us to take control of our nighttime routines. Sleep disorders can manifest in various forms, each with its distinct characteristics and implications for overall health.
By recognizing these conditions, busy people can make informed decisions to improve their sleep quality, leading to enhanced productivity and well-being.

One of the most prevalent sleep disorders is insomnia, which affects millions of

individuals worldwide. Insomnia is characterized by difficulty falling asleep, staying asleep, or waking up too early without the ability to return to sleep. For busy people, the pressures of work and life often exacerbate insomnia, creating a vicious cycle of stress
and sleeplessness. Identifying the signs of insomnia, such as prolonged wakefulness, fatigue during the day, and irritability, can help individuals seek appropriate solutions to enhance their sleep hygiene.

Another common disorder is sleep apnea, which involves interruptions in breathing during sleep. This condition can lead to fragmented sleep, causing excessive daytime sleepiness and difficulty concentrating. Busy individuals may overlook sleep apnea due to their hectic schedules, mistakenly attributing fatigue to a demanding lifestyle.
Recognizing symptoms like loud snoring, gasping for air during sleep, or persistent fatigue can prompt individuals to consult healthcare professionals for assessments and potential treatments that can restore their nightly rest.

Restless legs syndrome (RLS) is another condition that can significantly disrupt sleep. Characterized by uncomfortable sensations in the legs and an irresistible urge to move them, RLS often worsens during periods of inactivity or at night. This disorder can be particularly troublesome for busy people who may already struggle with winding down after a long day. Identifying RLS symptoms—such as an uncomfortable feeling in the legs, especially during evening hours—can lead to lifestyle adjustments or medical interventions that promote a more peaceful night's sleep.

Finally, understanding the impact of circadian rhythm disorders is essential. These disorders occur when the body's internal clock is out of sync with the external environment, resulting in difficulties falling asleep or waking up at desired times. For busy individuals who frequently travel or work irregular hours, this misalignment can lead to chronic sleep issues. Recognizing signs such as difficulty adjusting to new sleep schedules or feeling alert at night can help individuals take proactive steps to realign their circadian rhythms, such as utilizing light therapy or maintaining consistent sleep schedules.

By identifying and understanding these common sleep disorders, busy people can take meaningful steps toward improving their sleep quality and overall health. Recognizing the signs and symptoms of these conditions allows individuals to seek appropriate help, whether through lifestyle changes or professional guidance. As we delve deeper into effective relaxation techniques in this book, awareness of these disorders will serve as a foundation for transforming nighttime routines and achieving the restful sleep necessary for a busy life.

When to Seek Professional Help

When navigating the demands of a busy lifestyle, it can be all too easy to overlook the signs that indicate the need for professional help regarding relaxation and sleep. Many individuals may attribute sleepless nights to stress or a hectic schedule, but persistent difficulties in falling asleep or staying asleep can signal deeper issues. Recognizing when to seek help is crucial to maintaining both mental and physical health. If you find that your sleep problems are impacting your daily life, it is time to consider reaching out to a professional.

One key indicator that professional help may be necessary is the duration and severity of your sleep issues. If you consistently struggle to fall asleep for more than a few weeks, or if you wake up frequently throughout the night, these could be symptoms of sleep disorders such as insomnia or sleep apnea. Additionally, if your inability to relax and sleep is accompanied by feelings of anxiety, depression, or overwhelming stress, it is essential to consult with a healthcare provider. Ignoring these symptoms can lead to a downward spiral affecting your overall well-being and productivity.

Another key factor to consider is the effectiveness of your current relaxation techniques. Busy individuals often rely on quick fixes, such as over-the-counter sleep aids or excessive caffeine consumption, to combat fatigue. However, if you find that these methods are no longer working or are causing additional health issues, it may be time to seek professional guidance. A sleep specialist or therapist can provide tailored strategies and tools, helping you develop healthier habits that promote deeper and more restorative sleep.

In addition to persistent sleep issues, lifestyle changes can also indicate the need for professional help. If you have recently experienced significant changes in your life—such as a new job, loss of a loved one, or a major life transition—and find that your ability to relax and unwind has been severely disrupted, professional support can be invaluable.
Therapists and counselors can help you process these changes and develop coping strategies that facilitate relaxation and improve sleep quality.

Finally, if you notice that your sleep difficulties are impacting your relationships or work performance, seeking professional help becomes even more critical. Chronic sleep deprivation can lead to irritability, decreased concentration, and reduced productivity, all of which can strain personal and professional relationships. By addressing these issues with a professional, you can gain insights into the underlying causes of your sleep problems and develop a comprehensive plan for recovery. Prioritizing your mental health and sleep is not just beneficial for you; it can also enhance your interactions with those around you, leading to a more balanced and fulfilling life.

Natural Remedies for Sleep Issues

In the quest for restful sleep, busy individuals often overlook the power of natural remedies that can effectively promote relaxation and improve sleep quality. Unlike pharmaceutical options, which can have unwanted side effects and lead to dependency, natural remedies offer a gentle and holistic approach to addressing sleep issues. By incorporating certain herbs, dietary changes, and lifestyle adjustments, those with hectic schedules can find relief from insomnia and establish a more consistent sleep routine.

Herbal remedies have been used for centuries to promote sleep and relaxation. One of the most well-known options is chamomile, a mild sedative that can help to calm the mind and body. Drinking chamomile tea before bed can signal to your body that it is time to wind down, making it easier to fall asleep. Another effective herb is valerian root, which has been shown in studies to reduce the time it takes to fall asleep and improve sleep quality. For busy people looking for a quick fix, herbal supplements can be an easy addition to their nightly routine, ensuring they can de-stress after a long day.

In addition to herbal remedies, dietary adjustments can also play a crucial role in promoting better sleep. Foods rich in magnesium, such as leafy greens, nuts, and seeds, help to relax muscles and calm the nervous system. Consuming a small snack that includes both carbohydrates and protein, like whole-grain crackers with cheese, can stabilize blood sugar levels and prevent nighttime awakenings. It is also essential to be mindful of caffeine and sugar intake throughout the day, as these can interfere with the ability to fall asleep at night. By making conscious choices about what to eat, busy individuals can create an environment conducive to sleep.

Creating a calming bedtime routine is another natural remedy that busy people can adopt to improve their sleep quality. Engaging in relaxation techniques, such as deep breathing exercises, meditation, or gentle yoga, can significantly reduce tension and anxiety. These practices not only prepare the body for sleep but also help clear the mind of racing thoughts that often accompany a hectic lifestyle. Establishing a consistent bedtime routine signals to your body that it's time to transition from the demands of the day to a more restful state, making it easier to drift off into a deep sleep.

Finally, the importance of creating a sleep-friendly environment cannot be overstated. Keeping the bedroom dark, quiet, and cool can enhance the body's natural sleep cycles. Consider using blackout curtains, earplugs, or a white noise machine to block out distractions. Additionally, incorporating calming scents, such as lavender or sandalwood, can further promote relaxation. By combining these natural remedies, busy individuals can take proactive steps to address their sleep issues and cultivate a restorative nighttime routine that supports their overall well-being.

Chapter 10: Long-Term Strategies for Relaxation

Building a Sustainable Relaxation Practice

Building a sustainable relaxation practice is essential for busy individuals who often find themselves overwhelmed by the demands of daily life. Establishing a routine that prioritizes relaxation can significantly enhance your ability to unwind, leading to improved sleep quality and overall well-being. A sustainable practice involves not only the techniques you choose but also the commitment to making relaxation a regular part of your life. By integrating these practices into your daily schedule, you can create a reliable foundation for relaxation that fits seamlessly into your busy lifestyle.

To begin, consider identifying specific times in your day dedicated to relaxation. This may involve setting aside a few minutes in the morning before the day's responsibilities begin or carving out time in the evening to unwind. Consistency is key; by establishing a regular schedule, your body and mind will begin to recognize these moments as essential. Start with small increments of time—perhaps five to ten minutes—and gradually increase as you become more comfortable. The goal is to create a habit that does not feel overwhelming but instead becomes a cherished part of your routine.

Incorporating relaxation techniques that resonate with you personally is crucial for sustaining your practice. Explore various methods such as deep breathing exercises, progressive muscle relaxation, or guided imagery to find what feels most effective. For those looking to fall asleep faster, practices like mindfulness meditation or gentle yoga can be particularly beneficial. Experiment with different approaches, and do not hesitate to mix and match; the key is to discover a combination that helps you release tension and prepare your mind for rest.

Creating a conducive environment for relaxation can also enhance the effectiveness of your practice. Designate a quiet space in your home where you can retreat for relaxation sessions. This area should be free from distractions and clutter, allowing you to focus solely on unwinding. Consider incorporating elements that promote a calming atmosphere, such as soft lighting, soothing scents, or comfortable seating. By establishing a physical space dedicated to relaxation, you signal to your brain that it is time to power down and shift gears, making it easier to transition into a relaxed state.

Finally, it is important to remain flexible and patient with yourself as you develop your relaxation practice. Life can be unpredictable, and some days may not allow for the ideal relaxation experience. Acknowledge that setbacks are a natural part of the process, and instead of becoming discouraged, use them as opportunities for growth. Celebrate your progress, no matter how small, and remember that the ultimate goal is to build a practice that supports your well-being. By committing to a sustainable relaxation practice, you will not only enhance your ability to fall asleep faster but also cultivate a sense of peace and balance in your busy life.

The Role of Gratitude and Positivity

Gratitude and positivity play pivotal roles in fostering relaxation and improving overall well-being, particularly for busy individuals seeking to unwind and fall asleep faster. In today's fast-paced world, where stress and anxiety are prevalent, cultivating a mindset centered around gratitude can significantly shift one's perspective. This shift not only helps in alleviating negative thoughts but also promotes a sense of peace and contentment, which are essential for a good night's sleep. Understanding the mechanics behind gratitude and positivity can empower busy people to incorporate these practices into their nightly routines.

Research has consistently shown that practicing gratitude can lead to reduced levels of stress and anxiety. When individuals take the time to acknowledge the positive aspects of their day, it creates a mental buffer against the overwhelming pressures of daily life.
Engaging in gratitude exercises, such as journaling or simply reflecting on three things they are thankful for, can help busy people reframe their experiences. This practice encourages a focus on the positive rather than dwelling on stressors, making it easier to transition into a state of relaxation before bedtime.

Positivity is equally important in the quest for rapid relaxation. A positive mindset not only influences how we perceive our environment but also affects our physiological state. When we cultivate positive thoughts, our bodies respond by releasing hormones that promote relaxation and well-being, such as oxytocin and serotonin. Busy individuals can benefit from incorporating positive affirmations or visualizations into their evening routines. By focusing on uplifting thoughts, they can reduce the mental chatter that often interferes with falling asleep, thereby enhancing their ability to unwind after a long day.

Moreover, gratitude and positivity can create a ripple effect that extends beyond individual well-being. When busy people practice these qualities, they often influence those around them, fostering a more positive environment at home and at work. This communal positivity can further decrease stress levels, creating a collective atmosphere conducive to relaxation. For those who find it challenging to slow down, surrounding themselves with positive influences and expressing gratitude can serve as powerful catalysts for change, improving not only their own sleep patterns but also the dynamics of their relationships.

In conclusion, integrating gratitude and positivity into the lives of busy individuals is essential for achieving rapid relaxation and better sleep. By recognizing the benefits of these practices, busy people can develop healthier coping mechanisms that counteract the stressors of their daily lives. As they cultivate a mindset rooted in gratitude and positivity, they will likely find it easier to unwind at the end of the day, paving the way for restorative sleep and improved overall well-being. Embracing these practices is not just a step toward better sleep; it is an investment in a more balanced and fulfilling life.

Staying Committed to Your Relaxation Goals

Staying committed to your relaxation goals is essential for busy individuals who often find it challenging to carve out time for themselves. In a world that constantly demands attention, prioritizing relaxation may feel like a luxury rather than a necessity. However, this mindset can undermine your well-being, leading to increased stress and decreased productivity. To truly harness the benefits of relaxation, it is important to establish a commitment to your goals. This commitment will serve as a foundation for creating a more balanced life, allowing you to fall asleep faster and improve your overall health.

Establishing clear and attainable relaxation goals is the first step toward commitment. Consider what relaxation means to you and identify specific practices that resonate with your lifestyle. Whether it is dedicating 15 minutes at the end of the day for deep breathing exercises, practicing mindfulness, or engaging in light stretching, setting these goals makes them more actionable. Write them down and incorporate them into your daily routine. By visualizing your goals and making a conscious effort to achieve them, you lay the groundwork for lasting change in your relaxation habits.

To maintain your commitment, consider creating a supportive environment that encourages relaxation. This can include decluttering your space, minimizing distractions, and creating a designated relaxation area. Design elements such as comfortable seating, calming colors, and soothing scents can enhance your ability to unwind. Additionally, consider setting specific times during the day for relaxation. Consistency is crucial; by scheduling these moments into your calendar, you treat them with the same importance as work meetings or social obligations. Over time, this practice will help reinforce your commitment and make relaxation a natural part of your routine.

Accountability can also play a significant role in staying committed to your relaxation goals. Sharing your intentions with friends, family, or colleagues can create a sense of responsibility that encourages you to stay on track. You might even consider partnering with someone who shares similar goals, allowing you to support each other in your relaxation journeys. Regular check-ins can help keep both parties motivated and provide an opportunity to exchange tips and strategies. This sense of community can be invaluable, especially for busy people who may struggle to prioritize self-care.

Finally, be patient and compassionate with yourself as you work towards your relaxation goals. Life can be unpredictable, and there will be days when your commitment is tested. Rather than viewing setbacks as failures, treat them as opportunities to learn and adjust your approach. Reflect on what might have hindered your progress and seek ways to overcome those obstacles. Remember that relaxation is a skill that requires practice and dedication. By staying committed and flexible, you will find that the benefits of relaxation— like falling asleep faster and feeling more energized—will gradually become a natural part of your busy life.

Chapter 11: Resources and Tools

Apps and Gadgets for Better Sleep

The hustle and bustle of daily life can often lead to sleepless nights. Technology emerges as a powerful ally in the quest for better sleep. Numerous apps and gadgets are specifically designed to help busy individuals unwind and transition into restful slumber more quickly. By leveraging these modern tools, people can create an environment conducive to sleep, track their sleep patterns, and even practice relaxation techniques that pave the way for a more rejuvenating rest.

One of the most popular types of sleep aids are smartphone apps that focus on relaxation and sleep improvement. Apps like Calm and Headspace offer guided
meditations, sleep stories, and soothing soundscapes that can help ease the mind after a hectic day. These applications are tailored to fit into a busy lifestyle, allowing users to engage in short sessions that can be easily integrated into a nightly routine. By incorporating just a few minutes of mindfulness or relaxation before bed, users can significantly enhance their ability to fall asleep faster.

In addition to apps, wearable gadgets have gained traction among those seeking to enhance their sleep quality. Devices such as fitness trackers and smartwatches not only monitor physical activity but also provide valuable insights into sleep patterns. By analyzing data such as sleep duration and quality, users can identify trends and make informed adjustments to their bedtime routines. Some devices even feature gentle wake-up alarms that mimic natural sunrise, helping users wake up feeling refreshed rather than groggy, which is essential for busy individuals who need to hit the ground running each morning.

Smart home technology can also play a crucial role in creating an optimal sleep environment. Smart lighting systems can gradually dim as bedtime approaches, signaling to the body that it is time to wind down. Additionally, smart thermostats can help maintain a comfortable sleep temperature, which is vital for falling asleep and staying asleep throughout the night. These technologies not only enhance the sleep environment but also require minimal effort from the user, making them ideal for those with a packed schedule.

Finally, it is important to highlight the role of sound in promoting better sleep. Gadgets such as white noise machines or sleep sound generators can mask disruptive noises, creating a serene atmosphere conducive to falling asleep. These devices often come with various sound options, including nature sounds, ambient music, or white noise, allowing users to choose what works best for them. By investing in these apps and gadgets, busy individuals can take proactive steps toward achieving better sleep, ultimately enhancing their overall well-being and productivity in their daily lives.

Books and Podcasts on Relaxation

Finding moments of relaxation can seem like an elusive goal, especially for busy individuals. However, leveraging the right resources can make a significant difference in your ability to unwind and fall asleep faster. Books and podcasts focused on relaxation techniques provide valuable insights and tools that can help you integrate calming practices into your daily routine. This subchapter explores some of the most effective resources available, making it easier for you to tap into relaxation and improve your sleep quality.

Books on relaxation often offer structured approaches, combining scientific research with practical tips that busy individuals can easily incorporate into their lives. Titles such as "The Relaxation Response" by Herbert Benson introduce readers to the concept of a physiological state that counters stress. This book provides not just theory but also step- by-step instructions on how to elicit this relaxation response through techniques like deep breathing and visualization. Another excellent resource is "Wherever You Go, There You Are" by Jon Kabat-Zinn, which emphasizes mindfulness as a tool for relaxation. His teachings guide readers to practice being present, which can alleviate the racing thoughts that often accompany a busy lifestyle.

Podcasts have emerged as a popular medium for accessing relaxation techniques and insights. They offer the flexibility to listen while commuting, exercising, or unwinding at home. One standout is "Sleepy Time Mumbles," which features soothing stories designed to lull listeners into a state of relaxation. The gentle narration and calming themes can help busy minds transition from a hectic day to a peaceful night. Another noteworthy podcast is "The Daily Meditation Podcast," hosted by Mary Meckley. Each episode includes guided meditations that focus on different themes, making it easy for listeners to find a session that resonates with their current state of mind.

In addition to books and podcasts, it is important to consider how these resources can be integrated into your routine for maximum benefit. For example, reading a chapter from a relaxation book before bedtime can set the stage for a more peaceful night's sleep.

Alternatively, listening to a calming podcast episode during your evening wind-down can help signal to your body that it is time to relax. Establishing a ritual around these practices can create a sense of comfort and predictability, both of which are conducive to falling asleep faster.

The journey to relaxation is highly personal, and the resources you choose should reflect your preferences and lifestyle. Whether you gravitate toward the structured guidance found in books or the accessible, on-the-go nature of podcasts,

both mediums offer a wealth of knowledge to assist in managing stress. By exploring and utilizing these resources, busy individuals can take significant strides toward achieving a more relaxed state of mind, paving the way for improved sleep and overall well-being.

Professional Services to Consider

In the fast-paced world where busy people often find themselves juggling multiple responsibilities, the importance of prioritizing relaxation cannot be overstated.
Understanding the need for effective methods to unwind, various professional services have emerged to assist individuals in achieving quicker and deeper sleep. This subchapter will explore several professional services that can help you power down effectively, allowing you to reclaim your rest and recharge for the demands of daily life.

One of the most popular professional services available is massage therapy. This ancient practice has been shown to reduce muscle tension and promote relaxation, which can significantly aid in the transition to sleep. Therapists utilize various techniques such as Swedish, deep tissue, or aromatherapy massages to cater to individual needs. Regular sessions can lead to decreased stress levels, improved circulation, and a more restful night's sleep. For busy individuals, scheduling a massage on a weekly or bi-weekly basis can create a dedicated time for relaxation, making it easier to unwind after a hectic week.

Another valuable service to consider is guided meditation or mindfulness training. Many busy people struggle to quiet their minds at the end of the day, which can hinder their ability to fall asleep. Professional instructors can provide personalized sessions that teach techniques for calming the mind and body. This practice not only promotes relaxation but also helps individuals develop a routine of mental discipline that extends beyond the meditation session. By incorporating these techniques into their nightly rituals, busy individuals can find it easier to transition from the chaos of the day to a state of restfulness.

Sleep consulting is a burgeoning field that specifically addresses sleep issues faced by busy people. Sleep consultants can provide tailored advice on sleep hygiene, environmental adjustments, and behavioral changes to enhance sleep quality. They often conduct thorough assessments to identify personal sleep challenges and develop customized strategies. With their expertise, consultants can help individuals create an optimal sleep environment, establish a consistent sleep schedule, and implement relaxation techniques that fit into their busy lifestyles.

Additionally, acupuncture is a holistic service that can contribute to improved sleep. This ancient Chinese practice involves inserting thin needles into specific points on the body to promote energy flow and balance. Many busy individuals have found relief from insomnia and anxiety through acupuncture, as it can help regulate the body's stress response and enhance overall well-being. By incorporating acupuncture sessions into their self-care routines, individuals can address underlying issues that may be affecting their ability to relax and fall asleep quickly.

Exploring these professional services can significantly enhance the ability to power down and achieve restful sleep. By investing in massage therapy, guided meditation, sleep consulting, or acupuncture, busy individuals can cultivate a personalized approach to relaxation that fits their lifestyle. Ultimately, prioritizing these services not only aids in falling asleep faster but also contributes to a healthier, more balanced life, allowing individuals to meet their daily demands with renewed energy and focus.

Chapter 12: Conclusion and Moving Forward

Reflecting on Your Journey to Relaxation

Reflecting on your journey to relaxation is a crucial step in enhancing your ability to unwind and fall asleep faster. In today's fast-paced world, where responsibilities and distractions vie for your attention, it is easy to overlook the importance of self-reflection. Taking time to assess your relaxation strategies not only helps you identify what works best for you but also reinforces your commitment to prioritizing relaxation in your daily routine.

Begin by considering the various relaxation techniques you have experimented with over time. Perhaps you have tried deep breathing exercises, progressive muscle relaxation, or mindfulness meditation. Reflect on how each method made you feel and how effective it was in helping you achieve a state of calm. By evaluating your experiences, you can determine which practices resonate most with you and deserve a more prominent place in your relaxation toolkit. This self-assessment enables you to tailor your approach to relaxation, making it more personal and effective.

Another aspect to reflect on is the environment in which you relax. The physical space you create can significantly impact your ability to unwind. Consider the lighting, temperature, and overall ambiance of your relaxation area. Does it invite a sense of peace, or does it feel cluttered and distracting? Reflecting on these environmental factors encourages you to make necessary adjustments that promote relaxation. A tranquil environment can serve as a powerful cue for your mind and body, signaling that it is time to slow down and prepare for rest.

Mindfulness and self-awareness play a pivotal role in achieving balance. Engaging in mindfulness practices—such as meditation, deep breathing exercises, or gentle yoga— can help individuals become more attuned to their thoughts and emotions. This heightened awareness allows for better management of stress and anxiety, which are often barriers to falling asleep. By recognizing when the mind is racing or when the body is tense, one can implement relaxation techniques to calm both mind and body.
Practicing mindfulness regularly fosters a sense of peace that can extend into the nighttime routine, creating an optimal environment for sleep.

Ultimately, embracing a balanced life is about making intentional choices that prioritize personal well-being. For busy individuals, this means recognizing that productivity should not come at the expense of health and happiness. As sleep becomes increasingly vital for overall health, understanding how to cultivate balance can lead to improved sleep quality and a greater sense of control over one's life. By integrating practical strategies, such as evaluating commitments, establishing routines, and practicing mindfulness, individuals can create a lifestyle that supports relaxation and makes falling asleep faster an achievable goal.

Additionally, think about your daily habits and their influence on your relaxation journey. Are you allowing enough time for yourself to decompress after a busy day? Do you engage in activities that truly nourish your mind and spirit, or do you often find yourself defaulting to mindless scrolling on your devices? Recognizing the patterns in your daily life can help you shift towards more restorative practices. By consciously choosing to engage in activities that foster relaxation, such as reading or gentle stretching, you can create a more conducive atmosphere for falling asleep.

Lastly, consider the emotional aspects of your relaxation journey. Reflect on any feelings of guilt or anxiety that may arise when you take time for yourself. Busy people often struggle with the notion that relaxation is a luxury rather than a necessity.

Acknowledging these feelings is the first step toward overcoming them. Embrace the idea that prioritizing relaxation not only benefits you but also enhances your productivity and overall well-being. By reframing your perspective, you can cultivate a healthier relationship with relaxation, leading to more restful nights and rejuvenated days.

Setting Future Relaxation Goals

Busy individuals often overlook the importance of relaxation, leading to heightened stress levels and diminished overall well-being. Setting future relaxation goals is a proactive approach to ensuring that you prioritize downtime in your life. By establishing clear and achievable objectives, you can create a roadmap that guides you toward better relaxation practices and improved sleep quality. This subchapter will explore how to effectively set these goals, enabling you to unwind more efficiently and fall asleep faster.

To begin setting your relaxation goals, it is essential to assess your current habits and identify areas for improvement. Take time to reflect on your daily schedule and pinpoint moments when you feel overwhelmed or fatigued. Consider how much time you currently dedicate to relaxation and sleep, and evaluate whether this is sufficient for your needs. By understanding your starting point, you can create realistic and attainable goals that align with your lifestyle and commitments. This self-assessment will also help you recognize patterns in your daily routine that contribute to stress, allowing you to address them directly.

Once you have a clear understanding of your current situation, it is time to establish specific relaxation goals. Aim for goals that are measurable and time-bound, such as committing to a nightly wind-down routine that includes 15 minutes of reading or meditation before bed. Additionally, you might set a goal to reduce screen time by an hour each evening to promote better sleep hygiene. By defining specific objectives, you can track your progress and hold yourself accountable, making it easier to integrate relaxation into your busy life.

To further enhance your relaxation goals, consider incorporating a variety of techniques that resonate with you. This could include exploring mindfulness practices, engaging in gentle stretching or yoga, or even dedicating weekends to nature walks and outdoor activities. Experimenting with different approaches will help you discover what works best for your individual needs, ultimately leading to a more satisfying relaxation experience. Remember that the journey toward achieving your goals can be just as valuable as the goals themselves, so remain open to adjustments and new methods as you progress.

Finally, it is crucial to revisit and revise your relaxation goals regularly. Life is dynamic, and your needs may change over time due to work commitments, personal relationships, or shifts in health. By periodically assessing your relaxation objectives, you can ensure they remain relevant and effective. This ongoing evaluation allows you to celebrate your successes and refine your strategies, making relaxation an integral part of your life. By setting and adjusting your relaxation goals, you can cultivate a sustainable practice that not only helps you fall asleep faster but also enhances your overall quality of life.

Embracing a Balanced Life

The concept of balance often feels elusive, especially for busy individuals juggling multiple responsibilities. Embracing a balanced life is not merely about dividing time equally among work, family, and leisure; it involves prioritizing well-being and establishing a harmonious relationship between all aspects of life. This balance is essential, particularly for those seeking to enhance their ability to fall asleep faster. When life feels chaotic, the mind becomes overactive, making restful sleep an arduous challenge. Thus, understanding how to cultivate balance is crucial for achieving relaxation and improving sleep quality.

To embrace a balanced life, it is vital to assess current commitments and identify areas that may be overwhelming. Busy individuals often overload their schedules, leading to stress and fatigue. By taking a step back and evaluating daily activities, one can pinpoint which tasks are essential and which can be delegated, postponed, or eliminated. This process not only reduces the mental load but also creates space for relaxation and self- care—two components that are often neglected in the pursuit of productivity. When the mind is less cluttered, it becomes easier to unwind and prepare for restful sleep.

Establishing routines can significantly contribute to a balanced lifestyle. Routines provide structure, which can mitigate the chaos of a busy day. Incorporating consistent sleep hygiene practices—such as going to bed and waking up at the same time, creating a calming bedtime ritual, and limiting screen time before sleep—can help signal to the body that it is time to rest. Additionally, developing routines for work and leisure can ensure that neither aspect dominates one's life. By setting aside dedicated time for relaxation, hobbies, and social interactions, busy individuals can foster a sense of fulfillment, making it easier to disconnect from the day's stresses when it is time to sleep.